100

THINGS TO DO IN
BOSTON
BEFORE YOU
DIE

2nd Edition

100

THINGS TO DO IN
BOSTON
BEFORE YOU
DIE

• •

KIM FOLEY MacKINNON

REEDY PRESS

Library of Congress Control Number: 2018945640

ISBN: 9781681061719

Design by Jill Halpin

Cover Image: Kim Foley MacKinnon

All images are by Kim Foley MacKinnon, unless otherwise noted.

Printed in the United States of America
18 19 20 21 22   5 4 3 2 1

Please note that websites, phone numbers, addresses, and company names are
subject to change or cancellation. We did our best to relay the most accurate
information available, but due to circumstances beyond our control, please do not
hold us liable for misinformation. When exploring new destinations, please do your
homework before you go.

DEDICATION

For Rob and Sadie with love, as always.

CONTENTS

• •

Music and Entertainment

• •

• •

Culture and History

• •

Shopping and Fashion

PREFACE

Boston is a city of fascinating contradictions. You might think a city with such a long and important history might be stuck in the past, but while Boston is fiercely proud of its heritage, it is always looking ahead. Over the twenty-five years I've lived here, it's been exciting to see the changes, from the world-class chefs who have put us on the culinary map to the gorgeous Rose Kennedy Greenway that rose from the Big Dig construction project.

Oddly enough, one hundred things can seem like a big number and a small one at the same time. When I first started writing this book, it seemed overwhelming, but I found that when I went to narrow down my Boston picks to just one hundred, it hardly seemed like enough! I had a really difficult time choosing just one hundred things to feature. What you'll find in these pages is just the tip of the iceberg, but it's an excellent start.

While I've included classic Boston experiences like riding on the Swan Boats in the Public Garden, even locals might be surprised to learn that there is a secret steakhouse hidden in plain sight and that you can enter a lottery to ride on the USS *Constitution* on the Fourth of July. I've also included places that seem like tourist traps but actually deserve some love, and with good cause. New and old, side by side, that's what makes Boston a great city to live in and to explore.

• •

I'd love to hear about your experiences with my choices and I'd especially welcome your ideas and discoveries! Look for me on Instagram and Twitter @escapewithkim and tag your own Boston adventures at #100ThingsBoston.

ACKNOWLEDGMENTS

No book is ever the work of one person. I owe a big thank you to the friends and family I hit up for ideas, who offered me advice and encouragement and who ate and drank and explored with me as I researched what should be included in this book. I am also fortunate enough to have worked with many outstanding public relations people in Boston over the years and am eternally grateful for their help and hospitality.

Photo credit: Pixabay

FOOD AND DRINK

SPOON UP SOME CHOWDER
AT LEGAL SEA FOODS

One of New England's most well-known restaurants, Legal Sea Foods, has pretty humble beginnings. The first Legal opened in 1968, next to the Berkowitz family's fish market (which opened in 1950). The rest, as they say, is history. Still family run, Legal now has restaurants up and down the East Coast, and its famous clam chowder has been served at every presidential inauguration since 1981. There are any number of Legals in Boston, but the most scenic is its flagship restaurant, Legal Harborside, located on the waterfront. Head up to the third-floor, four-season rooftop lounge for a drink and some excellent chowder, where a glass roof and walls (retractable in warm weather) provide gorgeous views of the city and the harbor.

270 Northern Ave., 617-477-2900
legalseafoods.com

INDULGE IN SEAFOOD
AT B&G OYSTERS

Barbara Lynch, one of Boston's culinary superstars, has restaurants and bars scattered across the city, but this beautiful seafood bar in the South End is one of the more stylish places around town to fill up on oysters, lobster, and other seafood delights. Located below street level, the restaurant has an intimate feel, and the much-coveted outdoor garden patio is a hot ticket in the summer. A perfect night out can be as easy as selecting a variety of oysters from the ever-changing list, paired with a prosecco or a glass of crisp white wine, and simply enjoying the scene.

550 Tremont St., 617-423-0550
bandgoysters.com

SLURP UP SOME OYSTERS
AT UNION OYSTER HOUSE

The Union Oyster House is a tourist attraction for a reason: Not only is it a fun place to eat, it's also an awesome experience. The National Historic Landmark, which the National Park Service designated as the oldest continually run restaurant and oyster bar in the United States, is definitely worth a visit. My favorite thing to do is to sit at the oyster bar and chat with the longtime shuckers, some of whom have been there for decades. Get them talking and you'll be entertained for hours. And you'd be in good company too: diners over the years include a who's who of the famous, including Franklin Roosevelt, John F. Kennedy, and Bill Clinton, as well as governors, athletes, and movie stars.

41 Union St., 617-227-2750
unionoysterhouse.com

HEAD TO THE SOURCE
AT ISLAND CREEK OYSTERS

Delicious Island Creek oysters show up on menus across the city, including at the company's namesake restaurant in Kenmore Square, but for an up-close-and-personal look at where they come from, as well as all the oysters you can eat, you'll need to head to Duxbury. The comprehensive, not to mention entertaining, tour takes you to the hatchery, where you learn all about aquaculture before heading out onto Duxbury Bay by boat to see where the oysters finish growing. As you cruise around the bay, a staffer shucks as many oysters as you can eat. Seriously. My group of four easily downed at least two dozen a person. The tour is BYOB, so don't forget a bottle of your favorite wine. ICO also opened a beer garden and oyster bar at its eleven-acre waterfront property in 2018, another excellent way to enjoy their oysters.

397 Washington St., Duxbury
shop.islandcreekoysters.com/pages/farm-tours

DOWN A DOG
AT SULLIVAN'S

When the weather starts to warm up, a trip to Sullivan's at Castle Island is a Boston rite of spring. Located on Castle Island, the food stand, which has been serving up burgers, hot dogs, fries, and ice cream as well as seafood favorites since 1951, is a local favorite. The popular spot is still owned and operated by the Sullivan family, and generations of other families have made eating there a tradition. Line up for your order, then head out to a park bench to take in the views and watch the planes coming and going from Logan Airport. It's the perfect cheap date and an easy way to entertain the kids.

2080 William J. Day Blvd., 617-268-5685
sullivanscastleisland.com

DINE IN ELEGANCE
AT EASTERN STANDARD

Located in the Hotel Commonwealth in Kenmore Square, Eastern Standard sets the standard for elegance in this once somewhat seedy neighborhood. Evoking another era, the restaurant features a gorgeous long white marble bar running almost the length of the room, with red leather stools, cozy banquettes, and a large beautiful dining room. Cocktails are serious business here, and it is fun to sit at the bar and see the pros show off their skills. The restaurant serves several iconic dishes, but the favorite has to be the baked rigatoni with lamb and pork sausage and ricotta, which has been on the menu since day one and would probably incur a riot from patrons if it were ever removed.

528 Commonwealth Ave., 617-532-9100
easternstandardboston.com

DIG IN TO A STEAK
AT GRILL 23

Like any big city, Boston has its share of steakhouses, but what other cities don't have is a Grill 23, a one-of-a-kind locally owned steakhouse. Grill 23 has a unique relationship with Brandt Beef, a farm in California that raises vegetarian-fed, hormone-free, and antibiotic-free beef. One bite of a steak here, like the fourteen-ounce dry-aged prime New York strip, and you can taste the difference. There are all the usual steakhouse standards, with white tablecloths, a great wine list, and excellent service, so no need to worry on that front. Both seafood and produce are sourced locally, another thing that makes this steakhouse more than just a steakhouse. Whatever you do, don't leave without ordering the coconut cake—it's divine!

161 Berkeley St., 617-542-2255
grill23.com

DRINK IN SOME HISTORY
AT DOYLE'S

Boston is filled with historic Irish pubs, but most don't have a thing on Doyle's. Since 1882, this Jamaica Plain establishment has been serving up pints to the neighborhood and Boston's movers and shakers—most politicians make this a stop on the campaign trail. It's fun to walk around the bar and restaurant to check out its collection of historic knickknacks. There's a whole room dedicated to John Fitzgerald, JFK's grandfather. St. Patrick's Day is a hoot here, with the Boston Police Gaelic Column of Pipes and Drums usually making an appearance.

3484 Washington St., 617-524-2345
doylescafeboston.com

SNEAK A PEEK
AT THE BLEACHER BAR

It can be hard, not to mention expensive, to score tickets to a Red Sox game, but this cool bar offers a sweet ringside seat to Fenway Park. Located beneath the bleachers of Fenway's centerfield on Lansdowne Street, the Bleacher Bar has a feature no other bar has: a garage door-style window that looks right into the stadium. Formerly, the space was the visiting team's batting cage, so you feel like you're practically part of the action. Now fans jockey for prime seats in the bar to watch the game with cold beers and snacks. Even if there's no game, the view of the field can't be beat.

82A Lansdowne St., 617-262-2424
bleacherbarboston.com

SAY THE PASSWORD
AT THE 140 SUPPER CLUB

Who doesn't love a secret? At the 140 Supper Club, just thirty diners are allowed into a hidden restaurant located one flight below the Fairmont Copley Plaza hotel. If you have the password, that is. A long-forgotten room at the hotel has been turned into a fabulous private dining room, and enjoying an evening there feels deliciously decadent. The dinner, which is served at a long communal table, includes a four-course prix fixe menu and wine pairing. The chef comes out to explain every course and chat. Call the hotel to get on the list.

The opulent and gorgeous hotel, built in 1912, was designed by the same architect who planned the Plaza in New York. It easily evokes another era, perfect for a secret club. Make sure to walk through the stunning lobby and think about having a pre- or post-dinner drink in the OAK Long Bar to soak up the ambiance.

138 St. James Ave., 617-267-5300
fairmont.com/copley-plaza-boston/dining/140-supper-club

SLIP INTO
A FEW SPEAKEASIES

If you like the idea of the secret supper club but can't get tickets or you just can't get enough of hidden gems, Boston has you covered. Yvonne's, in Downtown Crossing; Drink, in the Seaport District; and Wink & Nod, in the South End all channel a cool speakeasy vibe. Yvonne's even has a clever smokescreen. It is located down an alley, and access to it is through a door in what looks like a hair salon. All three bars have top-of-their-game bartenders and unusual décor and give you the feeling that you are definitely part of an exclusive clientele.

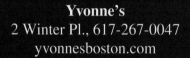

Yvonne's
2 Winter Pl., 617-267-0047
yvonnesboston.com

Drink
348 Congress St., 617-695-1806
drinkfortpoint.com

Wink & Nod
3 Appleton St., 617-482-0117
winkandnod.com

TAKE A TOUR
AT THE SAM ADAMS BREWERY

The Sam Adams brand is generally credited as kickstarting the craft brewery craze in the United States, so a visit to its Boston facility (the only one open to the public) is a must for beer-lovers. Located in Jamaica Plain, the brewery offers tours, a tap room, and a shop. At the tap room, you can try experimental beers the brewers are testing out that are not available anywhere else. Wednesday night is Brewers Flight Night, where the brewers pick out their favorites for you to try, and Thursday is Trivia Night, where you and your friends can pit your wits against other teams. The brewery also offers a variety of tours, from free one-hour overviews to more in-depth experiences for the true beer aficionado.

30 Germania St., 617-368-5080

samueladams.com

EAT YOUR WAY
THROUGH THE NORTH END

The North End, often referred to as Boston's "Little Italy," is a neighborhood simply packed with Italian restaurants, cafés, pizzerias, specialty grocers, shops, and more. The compact area has an embarrassment of foodie riches, and it can be hard to decide where to start. For almost twenty-five years, Michele Topor's North End Market Tours has been the go-to tour for learning all the ins and outs of the North End. Michele, or one of her excellent guides, takes you on a comprehensive trip around the neighborhood, stopping at locally owned spots to snack on delicious dishes, as well as talk about the history of the area and Italian food and culture. You'll go home with new knowledge, as well as a packet of recipes and restaurant recommendations.

617-475-3230
bostonfoodtours.com/north-end/

SIP A MARTINI
AT OAK LONG BAR

The OAK Long Bar + Kitchen has a special place in my heart, as it's where one of my favorite Boston fictional characters used to spend a lot of time. When I first moved to the city twenty-five years ago, I used Robert B. Parker's Spenser book series as my introduction to Boston. Spenser and his girlfriend spent many hours at the Oak Bar (as it used to be called), and I aspired to sip martinis in the exclusive bar one day, too. Now called the OAK Long Bar + Kitchen, the space looks a bit different from those days, but it is still the most elegant place in town to enjoy a perfectly made martini.

138 St. James Ave., 617-267-5300
oaklongbarkitchen.com

SAMPLE FINE WINES
AT THE BOSTON WINE FESTIVAL

The Boston Wine Festival, a feat masterminded and managed by Boston Harbor Hotel's chef Daniel Bruce, celebrates its thirtieth anniversary in 2019. The world-renowned event runs an astonishing three months, from January through March, with winemakers from around the globe hosting events from wine dinners to tastings. Highlights include a Grand Opening Reception and the Valentine's Champagne Dinner Dance.

70 Rowes Wharf, 617-330-9355
bostonwinefestival.net

INDULGE YOUR SWEET TOOTH
AT THE CHOCOLATE BAR

If Willy Wonka hosted a brunch, this is probably what it would look like. The extravagantly decadent, all-you-can-eat Saturday Chocolate Bar in Café Fleuri at the Langham, Boston hotel has been satisfying chocoholics for almost thirty years, every September through June. Each season has a different theme, but guests can count on more than one hundred different dessert combinations, from chocolate fountains to elaborate cakes to decorate-your-own doughnut stations. If you think there's never enough chocolate for you, this is a dream come true.

250 Franklin St., 617-451-1900
langhamhotels.com/en/the-langham/boston/dining/chocolate-bar

TASTE A SWEET PIECE OF HISTORY
AT PARKER HOUSE

The historic Omni Parker House Hotel, built in 1855, contains a lot of history within its four walls, but the tastiest is that this is where Boston's iconic dessert, the Boston cream pie, was first created (as well as the addictively delicious Parker House rolls). Head to the restaurant or bar to get a piece of where it all began. Word to the wise: it's not really a pie; it's more like a custard cake, but no matter, it's still delicious. Also, it's cool to note that Emeril Lagasse, Malcolm X, and Ho Chi Minh all worked here at one time or another.

Want to share the love? The hotel will deliver its iconic pie anywhere in the country. It is made fresh, then it's frozen and shipped directly from the bake shop to your door.

60 School St., 617-227-8600
omnihotels.com/hotels/boston-parker-house/dining/parkers-restaurant

ORDER A SLICE
AT SANTARPIO'S

Everyone has a favorite pizza joint in Boston, and Santarpio's in East Boston is on a lot of people's lists. Opened in 1903 as a bakery, with the addition of pizzas thirty years later, this family-owned restaurant has served up more pizzas than anyone could ever guess to legions of loyal fans. Its low prices are icing on the cake. An Italian cheese pizza will set you back just $9.50, while classics like the cheese, sausage, and garlic pie are just $13. Make sure to bring cash; they don't take credit cards.

111 Chelsea St., 617-567-9871
santarpiospizza.com

DRINK IN THE VIEWS
AT THE TOP OF THE HUB

Located on the fifty-second floor of the Prudential Center, the Top of the Hub is one of those spots that locals often ignore, but that's a shame. It offers one of the absolute best views of the city you can find, hands down, assuming it's a clear day. If you're not in the mood for dinner, head straight to the restaurant's jazz lounge, where for the price of a couple of drinks, you can enjoy the views and listen to jazz musicians, who perform every night of the week. This tends to be a special-occasion kind of place, so no flip-flops, hats, or shorts are allowed. It is a treat to go out to a place where people are dressed for the occasion.

800 Boylston St., Prudential Tower, 617-536-1775
topofthehub.net

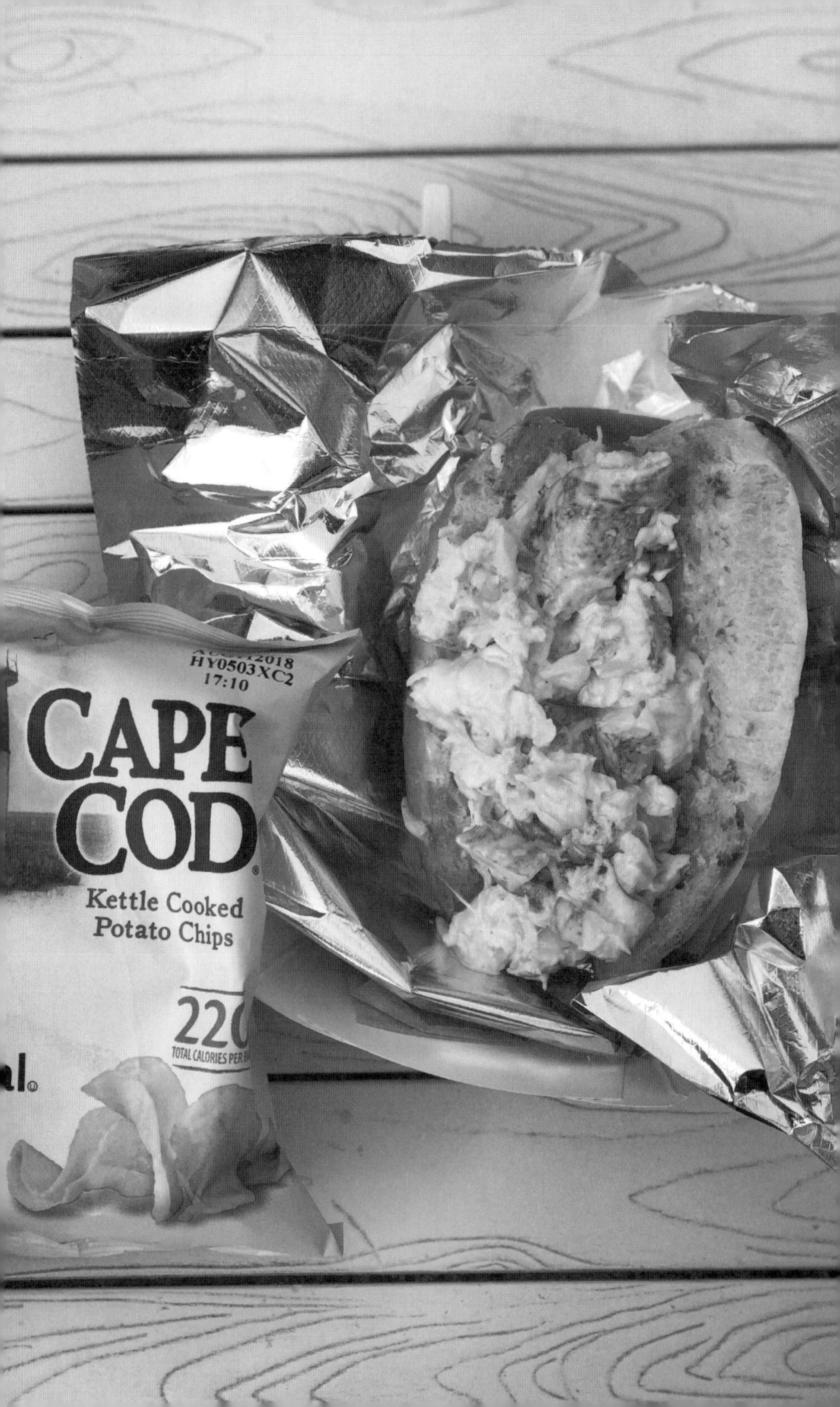
HY0503XC2
17:10
CAPE
COD
Kettle Cooked
Potato Chips

GET A LOBSTER ROLL
AT JAMES HOOK & CO.

Ask a group of locals where to get the best lobster roll in the city and you probably won't hear the same answer twice, but for a classic version, you can't beat old-school James Hook & Co. on the waterfront. The family-owned seafood company catches its own lobsters, distributing most of them to other businesses, but keeps enough back for those who want to get it at the source. They opt for a simple prep—a hot dog bun filled with fresh lobster meat, dressed in celery and mayo. You can taste how fresh it is—and don't bother getting a regular size. Order the large. It's that good. There are a few seats inside, but it can get crowded in there. You're better off sitting outside at one of the many picnic tables.

15–17 Northern Ave., 617-423-5501
jameshooklobster.com

EAT AT AN ICON
AT MARLIAVE

Walking into the Marliave is like stepping back in time. The black-and-white tile floors, the tin ceiling, and the Prohibition-era cocktails harken back to an earlier era when the historic restaurant opened. Henry Marliave, a French immigrant from Paris, opened his namesake restaurant in Downtown Boston in 1885, and though it has had its ups and downs over the years, it has been a neighborhood mainstay. Now owned and operated by Scott Herritt, who also owns the nearby Grotto restaurant, the menu skews toward French, with dishes like escargot, French onion soup, and steak frites. The twice-daily oyster happy hour, from 4 to 6 p.m. and again from 9 to 10 p.m., is a bargain and one more reason to visit.

10 Bosworth St., 617-422-0004
marliave.com

FEAST ON LOBSTER PIZZA
AT SCAMPO

What? Lobster is not just served on hot dog rolls? That's right, years ago legendary Boston chef Lydia Shire created this over-the-top pie, which boasts about two pounds of lobster meat, caramelized shallots, and garlic and is about as decadent as a pizza can get. It's a signature dish she's made at most of her restaurants over the years. Today, you can find it, and her, at Scampo at the Liberty Hotel. The restaurant's name means to "escape" in Italian, an apt moniker for a spot in a building that was, in a former life, the Charles Street Jail.

The jail, which was constructed in 1851, held such famous inmates as Mayor James Michael Curley, Malcolm X, and Sacco and Vanzetti. After closing in the 1990s and suffering years of neglect, the building was reborn as a gorgeous hotel in 2007, with some of its former architectural features restored or retained. Make sure to take a walk around the whole property.

215 Charles St., 617-536-2100
scampoboston.com

ORDER A COCKTAIL
IN A FORMER JAIL CELL

Before or after you dine on lobster pie, head to another unique spot in the Liberty Hotel—Alibi, a bar set in the former jail's drunk tank. Check out the original bluestone floors, brick cell walls, and iron bars on windows and doors, as well as funny celebrity mugshots on the walls. You can also enjoy a cocktail or snack outside in the jail's former exercise yard, which has been turned into a hip patio with a bar. Drinks have amusing names like Cool Hand Cuke, Single White Female, and Blood In Blood Out.

215 Charles St., 857-241-1144
alibiboston.com

SWIM AND SIP
AT THE ROOFTOP COLONNADE POOL

The city's only rooftop pool and bar is somewhat of a hidden gem. Many people think the Colonnade's pool, located twelve stories up, is just for hotel guests, but non-guests can buy day or evening passes to hang out every day except for Saturdays and Sundays (unless you rent a cabana). The pool is generally open from May through September and has a full bar, as well as a casual menu with dishes like lobster rolls and pizza. Special events, like Wednesday morning yoga, kickboxing classes, and local celebrity chef dinners, make for fun nights.

120 Huntington Ave., 617-424-7000
colonnadehotel.com/m/rooftop-pool

RAISE A GLASS TO HISTORY
AT WARREN TAVERN

The Warren Tavern, rebuilt in 1780, is said to be the oldest watering hole in the state. Famous regulars included George Washington and Paul Revere (he definitely got around). The building was one of the first to be constructed after the British burned down Charlestown (priorities). The pub is named after Dr. Joseph Warren, a friend of Revere's who was killed at the Battle of Bunker Hill. The Bunker Hill Monument is just steps away from the pub, making this a logical place to catch your breath and enjoy some refreshments, especially if you climbed to the top of the monument or have been trekking along the Freedom Trail.

2 Pleasant St., 617-241-8142

warrentavern.com

DOWN A PINT
AT J. J. FOLEY'S

A South End institution, J.J. Foley's has been around since 1909. It is the oldest continuously operated family-owned pub in the city (not to be confused with the oldest continuously run tavern or simply the oldest tavern or … oh, never mind, it doesn't matter). Legend has it that during Prohibition, the Irish pub fronted as a shoe store. This is definitely an old-school pub, with lots of wood and brass and no-nonsense bartenders who tell it like it is but pour a perfect pint. It's also a fun place to people watch and hang out with the locals, who also tell it like it is.

117 E. Berkeley St., 617-728-9101
jjfoleyscafe.com

天下為公

DINE ON DIM SUM
IN CHINATOWN

As with lobster rolls, every local has a favorite place for dim sum in Chinatown. As a resident, I'm trying to work my way through all the options one by one. At publication time, Hei La Moon was winning in my book (but truthfully, it's hard to go wrong anywhere around here). The restaurant is absolutely massive, which means you never have to wait long for a table, even on crowded weekends. And once seated, there is always, and I mean always, a cart of delicious items circling among the tables, from barbecue pork buns to shark fin dumplings to lotus seed buns. On top of that, it's a bargain to dine here. Even when my friends and I go absolutely nuts, ordering everything in sight, we are always shocked at how inexpensive our bill turns out to be. After you eat, make sure to wander through the neighborhood, checking out the shops and bakeries.

88 Beach St., 617-338-8813
heilamoon.com/menu_dim_sum.html

BRUNCH ON THE ROOFTOP
AT THE TAJ

The seasonal Rooftop Sunday Brunch at the Taj Boston hotel is what brunch should be. Perched seventeen floors up, diners get stunning views of the Public Garden served up along with tasty mimosas or Bloody Marys. An outstanding selection of dining options includes a raw bar, sushi bar, taco bar, made-to-order waffle and omelet stations, artisanal cheeses, carving stations, and—since this is a Taj property—creative Indian cuisine to boot. You'll want to save room for the amazing dessert buffet.

15 Arlington St., 617-536-5700
thetajboston.com

BOOK A TABLE
AT BOGIE'S PLACE

I love telling friends about this hidden steakhouse, tucked away behind a curtain in bustling jm Curley, an eatery in Downtown Crossing. Most people have no idea there's a secret twenty-seat oasis of calm just a step away, with cozy seats, a tiny bar, and a carefully curated menu with classic dishes like bone marrow, wedge salad, and porterhouse steaks. Order the Absinthe Fountain, served tableside, for a cool cocktail experience. You can't just walk in off the street, so make sure to book your table well in advance. Reservations fill up quickly. And cell photos and photography are a no-no. Some things should stay shrouded in a little mystery and romance, and thankfully, Bogie's is such a place.

25 Temple Pl., 617-338-5333
bogiesplace.com/adultsonly

GO ON A PUB CRAWL

Boston is full of so many pubs, we could devote a whole other book to them, but these three, located within a few blocks of each other, make for a fun self-guided tour on foot. Start at the Bell in Hand, which has been around since 1795. It was opened by Jimmy Wilson, who was Boston's town crier for fifty years, hence the name. Go around the corner (literally 125 feet away) to the Green Dragon, which originally opened in 1654 and served the likes of Paul Revere and John Hancock. Finish up at the Black Rose, a newcomer in terms of Boston (it opened in 1976), which is a five-minute walk away and offers live Irish music every night of the week.

Bell in Hand
45 Union St., 617-855-0061
bellinhand.com

Green Dragon
11 Marshall St., 617-367-0055
greendragonboston.com

Black Rose
160 State St., 617-742-2286
blackroseboston.com

Photo by Sean Marrinan

MUSIC AND ENTERTAINMENT

GET YOUR GROOVE ON
AT THE BEEHIVE

To enjoy live music every night of the week, head to this lively South End spot, which has no cover charge and offers excellent food and drinks. Located in the Boston Center for the Arts complex, the large, artsy, two-level restaurant/club is decorated with works from local artists. It offers lots of different spaces to kick back and take in the live entertainment, which might be jazz, blues, cabaret, burlesque, country, or R&B on any given night. There are normally two sets each night: one during the dinner hours, which is a bit chill, and then a later one, which ramps it up a notch. The eclectic menu offers everything from vegetable curry to duck au poivre. Jazz brunch on the weekends is also a great way to start off a Saturday or Sunday.

541 Tremont St., 617-423-0069
beehiveboston.com

OPEN YOUR EARS
AT THE BOSTON SYMPHONY HALL FOR THE BOSTON SYMPHONY ORCHESTRA

Gorgeous Symphony Hall opened on October 15, 1900, and is considered one of the top concert halls in the world. The perfect acoustics make listening to concerts performed by the Boston Symphony Orchestra, led by Latvian-born BSO music director Andris Nelsons, exquisite to experience. While you're in the hall, look for the sixteen replicas of Greek and Roman statues, which are all related in some way to music, art, or literature and for the Symphony Hall organ, an Aeolian Skinner designed by G. Donald Harrison. It was installed in 1949 and is considered one of the finest in the world. Free behind-the-scene tours are a great way to learn more. Or better yet, go to a live concert!

301 Massachusetts Ave., 617-266-1492

bso.org

WATCH A PLAY UNDER THE STARS
AT SHAKESPEARE ON THE COMMON

Now firmly established as a Boston summertime tradition, the annual Shakespeare on the Common production offers a chance to see the Commonwealth Shakespeare Company perform one of the Bard's great works, from *Romeo and Juliet* to *Richard III*, for free at Boston Common. Bring a blanket (or a low chair) and a picnic and prepare to be entertained. Or, if you prefer, take advantage of the many food trucks and vendors. If you simply must be up front, you can reserve seats in a limited Friends Section for sixty dollars pre-season, or seventy-five dollars during performance weeks. Shows usually run from mid-July through early August every night except Mondays.

Parkman Bandstand, Boston Common, 617-426-0863
commshakes.org/free-shakespeare-on-the-common

TAP YOUR TOES
AT WALLY'S CAFE JAZZ CLUB

This tiny spot is an absolute must for music fans. Ever since 1947, performers have been jamming at Wally's, which is open every night of the year. The historic family-owned club is considered a training ground for many aspiring music students attending local institutions like Berklee College of Music. They are happy to hone their craft where big names like Billie Holiday and Charlie Parker once made appearances.

Every night, there's an early jam session from 6 to 9 p.m., then another from 9:30 p.m. until 2 a.m. Bands perform jazz, funk, blues, or a mix. There's no cover charge and people from all over town squeeze into the small space to hear talented new performers who might just be the next big thing. It's one of Boston's more diverse scenes, and you never know who might drop in.

427 Massachusetts Ave., 617-424-1408
wallyscafe.com

CROON A LITTLE
AT THE SINATRA BRUNCH AT LUCKY'S

Lucky's Lounge is one of those spots you'd miss if you didn't know it was there, so I'm here to tell you not to miss it. This Southie hangout is accessed via a hard-to-spot, garden-level entrance in a brick building on Congress Street. On the menu, a slew of Sinatra-themed foods and drinks make ordering fun— try the Chairman of the Board, made with grilled tenderloin tips, two eggs, secret sauce, and brunch potatoes, and the Angel Eyes, a tasty concoction of cucumber vodka, yellow chartreuse, St. Germain, prosecco, and lemon juice. Live music is provided by the Ron Poster Duo featuring Alex MacDougall, who doesn't do a gimmicky impersonation of Ol' Blue Eyes but manages to channel his smooth tunes nonetheless.

355 Congress St., 617-357-5825
luckyslounge.com

CHANNEL A BYGONE ERA
AT SCULLERS JAZZ CLUB

Another local music institution is Scullers, which has featured big names like Harry Connick Jr., Tony Bennett, Christian Scott, Lisa Fischer, Michael Bublé, and Wynton Marsalis, as well as up-and-coming acts, since 1989. Some names you might know, like Diana Krall, Norah Jones, and Peter Cincotti, were introduced on Scullers' stage. Since the club is located on the ground floor of the DoubleTree Suites, you can make a night of it and enjoy dinner with the show. A three-course prix fixe menu is available, as well as a full bar. What's great about Scullers is that it feels like an old-time jazz club, where patrons dress up a bit and are seated at tables, all of which have great sight lines of the musicians.

400 Soldiers Field Rd., 866-777-8932
scullersjazz.com

YUK IT UP
AT IMPROV ASYLUM

This show is never the same twice, with a mix of sketch comedy and audience-assisted improv scenes, so get ready to enjoy some sidesplitting laughs. A show at Improv Asylum, located in the North End, plus an Italian dinner at one of the nearby restaurants, makes for a great night out. If you're up for a more ribald evening, plan to go to one of the raunchier midnight shows on the weekends, where nothing is off limits. The comedy troupe also features various theme nights, based on games like Cards Against Humanity or late-night talk shows, which mixes things up even more. The venue has a bar, so you can enjoy drinks before and during the show, which you might need if you get picked out by an actor for some good-humored roasting.

216 Hanover St., 617-263-6887
improvasylum.com

SING AT THE SUPPER CLUB
AT CAPO

South Boston has exploded with cool new restaurants and bars in the last few years, and Capo is one of the more popular, serving up Italian dishes with flair. But what sets the popular restaurant apart is its four-thousand-square-foot lounge in the basement, where you'll find the restaurant's Supper Club and free (yes, free) live entertainment several nights a week, from comedy acts to live bands and a Sinatra tribute band singing the classics. It doesn't take much to get the crowd up and moving to the music, so bring your dancing shoes!

443 W. Broadway, 617-993-8080
caposouthboston.com/supper-club

PLAY DETECTIVE
AT *SHEAR MADNESS*

For fans of interactive murder mystery dinners (like me), *Shear Madness* is a must. But instead of dining on mediocre food while actors juggle their characters (as well as your food) *Shear Madness* offers a different kind of experience in a legit theater. Don't worry, though—you and the rest of the audience still get to solve the crime of the comedy whodunit, which is set in a hairstyling salon in the city. The storyline is that the landlady who lives above the shop is murdered and everyone in the salon has a reason to do her in. The audience gets to question the actors and tries to solve the crime. The outcome is never the same and amazingly, the hilarious interactive show has been running since 1980.

Charles Playhouse, 74 Warrenton St., 617-426-5225
shearmadness.com

FUN FACT

Shear Madness is listed in the *Guinness Book of World Records* as the longest-running play in the history of the United States.

GET MESSY
AT THE BLUE MAN GROUP

While the Blue Man Group got its start in New York City in the 1980s, Boston was its first venture out of the city, and it has been playing continuously to enrapt crowds at the Charles Playhouse ever since 1995. The somewhat intense, and always entertaining, show is performed mostly in pantomime, except for the occasional voice-over. Front-row patrons are given ponchos to wear for protection from paint splatters and flying Jell-O. It's really hard to describe exactly what the show is like, but trust me, it's something you'll never forget.

Charles Playhouse, 74 Warrenton St., 800-BLUEMAN (258-3626)
blueman.com/boston

GET A TASTE OF THE SOUTH
AT THE HOUSE OF BLUES

House of Blues music venues are found across the country these days, but the very first one was founded across the river in Cambridge in a converted historic house in 1992. It moved over to the Boston side later. Isaac Tigrett created the original House of Blues with the aim to introduce the world to the music of the rural South, including blues, R&B, gospel, jazz, and roots-based rock and roll, which it still does to this day. While Boston's late-night scene can be, well, a little "sceney," the House of Blues offers a solid place to hear great bands. You can also get tasty Southern food at the bar and restaurant, which also serves up vegetarian dishes and other healthy options.

15 Lansdowne St., 888-693-2583
houseofblues.com/boston

DANCE THE NIGHT AWAY
AT CLUB CAFÉ

This South End hotspot, a restaurant, cabaret, and dance club all in one, has always got something going on, from drag bingo to trivia night to karaoke. For almost forty years, Club Café has been the center of Boston's gay community, with a social scene that welcomes everyone. Every Thursday, Friday, and Saturday night, a lively dance party starts at 10 p.m., and in the Napoleon Room, you'll find cabaret shows, cutting-edge performing artists, comedians, or musicians every night of the week. The all-you-can-eat Sunday brunch is a delicious deal.

209 Columbus Ave., 617-536-0966
clubcafe.com

CELEBRATE AMERICA'S BIRTHDAY
AT BOSTON HARBORFEST
WITH THE BOSTON POPS

A few days before the Fourth of July, Boston pulls out all the stops at Boston Harborfest, with hundreds of activities and events held all over the city, including historical reenactments, a chowder cookoff, Freedom Trail walks, boat tours, live entertainment, and much more. For more than three decades, this festival has been a summer highlight for locals and visitors alike.

On July Fourth, the not-to-miss Boston Pops Fireworks Spectacular at the Hatch Shell on the Esplanade is an extravaganza like no other. People come at dawn (some from across the country) to claim their spaces to hear the Boston Pops, and a variety of special guests like Dolly Parton and Rachel Platten perform while fireworks explode over the harbor. It really is spectacular!

617-439-7700
bostonharborfest.com

GO GREEN
ON ST. PATRICK'S DAY

At least once in your life, you should check out Boston's over-the-top St. Patrick's Day Parade, where more than half a million people come out to celebrate. And in Boston, not only is March 17th St. Patrick's Day, but it's also Evacuation Day, which marks the expulsion of the British regulars from the area, ending the Siege of Boston in 1776.

Head to South Boston early to claim your spot to watch the fife and drum players, marching bands, members of the armed forces, police, and politicians celebrating the neighborhood's longstanding Irish heritage. This is also people watching at its best, with enthusiastic spectators decked out in everything from green tutus to shamrock-painted faces. Word to the wise: more than a few people indulge early, so keep an eye out for rowdy groups.

Sunday closest to March 17

Start: Broadway Station, South Boston
Finish: Andrew Square, South Boston
844-478-7287
southbostonparade.org

CATCH A FLICK
AT THE COOLIDGE CORNER THEATRE

Boston doesn't have any independent movie theaters left, so fans of small theaters with character have to head further afield. My favorite is an easy subway ride from downtown Boston at the Coolidge Corner Theatre in Brookline, which has been showing art house and independent films since 1933. The charming theater was built as a church in 1906 and later redesigned as an Art Deco movie palace in 1933. Today, theatergoers can enjoy both classic and new movies, along with wine and beer and regular movie snacks. I've been to a showing of *The Princess Bride* where the audience was urged to speak the actors' lines aloud and a midnight showing of *The Rocky Horror Picture Show* where props were encouraged. Just try that at a chain theater!

290 Harvard St., Brookline, 617-734-2501
coolidge.org

SCARE UP SOME SPIRITS
ON A GHOSTS & GRAVESTONES TOUR

There are lots of ways to see Boston, but this delightfully creepy tour digs into Boston's scarier side. Leading you half the time on a trolley and half on foot, your ghostly tour guide takes you to infamous murder sites, haunted places, and two of the city's oldest burying grounds on your ninety-minute experience. You'll hear stories about the Boston Strangler, among many other unsavory characters; see where Bostonians used to hang criminals; and walk by the city's most haunted hotel, the Omni Parker House, to learn about its spookier guests. The tour is a bit campy, but what else would you expect from a ghost tour?

Runs April through mid-November.

866-754-9136
ghostsandgravestones.com/boston

LESS SPOOKY TOURS

Boston Duck Tours
617-267-3825
bostonducktours.com

Old Town Trolley
855-396-7433
trolleytours.com/boston

City View Trolley Tours
617-363-7899
cityviewtrolleys.com

SPORTS AND RECREATION

RIDE A GIANT SWAN
IN THE PUBLIC GARDEN

Chances are, even if you've never stepped foot in Boston, you've seen the iconic image somewhere of groups of happy people being rowed around a body of water in a giant swan in the center of the city. These celebrated boats are found in Boston's Public Garden, America's oldest botanical garden.

The historic Swan Boats have been gliding over the park's lagoon, under the scenic weeping willow trees and what's billed as the world's smallest suspension bridge, since 1877. No warm-weather visit to Boston is complete without taking a ride on these pedal boats (don't worry, a captain supplies the foot power). Elsewhere in the twenty-four-acre park, you'll encounter meandering paths, gorgeous gardens, beautiful flower beds, and sculptures of historic figures like George Washington. Don't miss the charming *Make Way for Ducklings* bronze sculptures, done by Nancy Schön as a tribute to the 1941 classic children's book of the same name written by Robert McCloskey.

Swan Boats run mid-April through mid-September.
The park is open year-round.

Public Garden, 4 Charles St., 617-522-1966
swanboats.com

TIP
The Friends of the Public Garden
offer free one-hour tours of the garden
three days a week from May
through September.

SKATE OR SPLASH
AROUND THE FROG POND

Adjacent to the Public Garden is Boston Common, which, founded in 1634, is the oldest public park in the United States. Locals used the space to graze their cattle until 1830. Over the years, it's been used to celebrate events (the repeal of the Stamp Act and the end of the Revolutionary War); punish criminals (there used to be a whipping post and stocks, not to mention a hanging tree); and stage public lectures and gatherings (Charles Lindbergh, Martin Luther King Jr., and Pope John Paul II all spoke here, to name a few of the greats).

Today, the fifty-acre park still serves as a giant backyard for the city, with all sorts of public events, from protests to concerts. The Frog Pond, one of its livelier features, is an ice-skating rink in the winter and a giant splash pool in the summer. While it's certainly fun for kids and families to cool off in the water when it's hot out, the Frog Pond really shines in winter. To take a spin on the ice, especially at night with the golden dome of the State House shining above you and twinkling lights in the trees, is magical.

Boston Common, Beacon and Park Sts., 617-635-2120
bostonfrogpond.com

JOIN THE (TREE) MOB
AT THE ARNOLD ARBORETUM

While it's hard to pick a favorite gem out of the Emerald Necklace, I am partial to the Arnold Arboretum, which is within walking distance of my house. I have spent countless hours wandering here. And there's a lot of space in which to wander—281 acres, to be exact. A great way to learn about the park is to join a "Tree Mob," an interactive tour led by scientists or other specialists at the Arnold Arboretum. The thirty-minute events are a chance to learn little-known facts about the living plant collection.

The highest point in the park is Bussey Hill, where you're rewarded with unbeatable views of Great Blue Hill and the Boston skyline. Every season offers its own delights, but spring is especially glorious. In May one of the country's most significant and fragrant lilac collections comes to life. Hordes of people visit on Mother's Day to picnic (the only day of the whole year this is allowed) and to literally smell the flowers. Be sure to check out the arboretum's website for details about guided tours and special events throughout the year.

125 Arborway, 617-524-1718
arboretum.harvard.edu

SNAP A PHOTO
ON ACORN STREET

This charming little street in Beacon Hill is said to be one of the most photographed streets in Boston (if not in the country) and with good reason. The one-block cobblestone road is too narrow for cars, so pedestrians are free to roam, but take care—the uneven road can be tricky to navigate. Street-proud residents take care to make sure their rowhouses' doors and window boxes are always looking picture-perfect. In spring and summer, flowerboxes overflow with colorful displays. In fall, pumpkins and other autumnal décor come out, and in winter, wreaths and twinkling lights make the street seem like something out of a fairy tale.

Acorn St., between W. Cedar and Willow Sts.

EXAMINE THE JEWELS
OF BOSTON'S EMERALD NECKLACE

Forget gemstones—Boston's Emerald Necklace is a long string of six delightful green spaces stretching seven miles from one end of the city to the other. Masterminded in the late nineteenth century by landscape architect extraordinaire Frederick Law Olmsted, who also happened to design New York's Central Park (among many other green spaces), the parks are composed of the Back Bay Fens, the Riverway, Olmsted Park, Jamaica Pond, Arnold Arboretum, and Franklin Park.

The interconnected parks were designed to give city dwellers relief from the hustle and bustle of town, a job that they fulfill to this day. From walking along shady paths to rowing on the pond to playing golf or visiting the zoo at Franklin Park, the Emerald Necklace offers countless ways to enjoy the outdoors. The Emerald Necklace Conservancy provides tours, maps, exhibits, and other info from its visitor center in the Back Bay Fens.

Shattuck Visitor Center, 125 The Fenway, 617-522-2700
emeraldnecklace.org

TIP

Are you a fan of Frederick Law Olmsted, like I am? Check out the Frederick Law Olmsted National Historic Site, where you can visit Fairsted, his Boston home and office, which he opened in 1883. The site is only open in the summer, but the extensive grounds are open year-round.

99 Warren St., Brookline, 617-566-1689
nps.gov/frla/index.htm

STOP AND SMELL THE FLOWERS
AT THE KELLEHER ROSE GARDEN

A jewel within a jewel, the Kelleher Rose Garden is located in the Back Bay Fens (part of Boston's Emerald Necklace string of parks designed by Frederick Law Olmsted in the 1880s). The hidden garden, designed in 1931, was a later addition. Today, it contains more than ten classes and two hundred varieties of roses, with almost 1,500 individual plants. It's easy to miss the garden, which is somewhat hidden behind a large yew hedge, but it's definitely worth seeking out to enjoy what feels like a secret garden.

Back Bay Fens, 617-522-2700
emeraldnecklace.org/venue/kelleher-rose-garden

DITCH
THE MAINLAND

Martha's Vineyard and Nantucket, two islands just off the coast of Cape Cod, offer different enticements to visit. The Vineyard, where the Obamas famously vacationed, is just seven miles from shore. The one-hundred-square-mile island boasts beautiful beaches, sea captains' homes, and plenty of diversions, from sailing to cycling.

Nantucket, located thirty miles from the Massachusetts coastline, is a bit more remote and exclusive and was once the whaling capital of the world. Upscale restaurants, stunning, uncrowded beaches, and historic homes make for a charming visit. Day-trippers can fly or take a ferry to either island, but if you can spare the time to spend a night, you'll get a chance to enjoy your island getaway that much more.

Steamship Authority
Woods Hole or Hyannis, 508-477-8600
steamshipauthority.com

Cape Air
Logan Airport, 800-227-3247
capeair.com

PLANE SPOT
AT CASTLE ISLAND

One of Boston's charmingly misnamed attractions, Castle Island is neither an island nor graced with a castle. Instead, you'll find a historic fort, great views, and even a few beaches. A bonus is that Sullivan's is also here, so if you're craving a hot dog or ice cream, you're all set for an impromptu picnic. Situated in South Boston, the twenty-two-acre park is actually connected to the mainland by causeways, and it's located just across the water from Logan International Airport, meaning it's a fantastic place to spot planes taking off and landing. They seem to soar right above your head, making for a thrilling experience.

William J. Day Blvd., 617-727-5290
mass.gov/dcr

TIP
Castle Island is a great place to see the USS *Constitution* do its annual turnaround on July Fourth.

SAIL OVER
TO THE BOSTON HARBOR ISLANDS

The Boston Harbor Islands are one of Boston's lesser-known attractions, despite being just a short ferry ride away from downtown. Once there, you can do everything from exploring old forts to swimming to hiking. You can visit the nation's oldest continually used light station; enjoy clambakes, live musical performances, vintage 1860s baseball games played by costumed teams; and even camp overnight on four of the islands. Finally, the views from the water and the islands offer an incomparable shot of Boston's scenic skyline.

Visitors tend to gravitate to two islands, Georges and Spectacle. Georges is home to the spooky Civil War-era Fort Warren, which is fun to explore (look out for the resident ghost, the Lady in Black). Spectacle Island, which has served as farmland, a quarantine hospital, a glue factory, a resort, and a landfill, now offers a beach (with lifeguards), 2.5 miles of trails, and the highest viewing point of any of the islands, at 155 feet.

Ferries run May through October. Even if all you have time for is a quick round trip, I can't recommend it enough.

Boston Harbor Islands, 617-223-8666
bostonharborislands.org

EXPLORE
THE ROSE KENNEDY GREENWAY

Forget about riding a horse on a carousel and ask yourself, where can I ride a codfish? Okay, maybe not you, but your kids (or you, vicariously) will enjoy the custom-made New England-centric carousel at the Rose Kennedy Greenway, which features a seal, a peregrine falcon, a sea turtle, a lobster, a green grasshopper, and a whimsical sea creature instead of the usual four-legged creatures.

The 1.5-mile-long park, which replaced the eyesore of an elevated highway, wends its way through several Boston waterfront neighborhoods. There is a LOT going on here, from farmers markets to beer gardens to food trucks to outdoor movies. There's also live music, temporary exhibits, edible herb gardens, seven splash fountains, and much, much more. Head on down and wander around. I guarantee you won't be bored. It always feels like you've stumbled into a super-cool block party, especially when it's warm outside and the city comes out to play.

617-292-0020
rosekennedygreenway.org

ROOT, ROOT, ROOT
FOR THE HOME TEAMS

No one could ever deny that Boston is a sports-crazed city. With the Boston Red Sox, the New England Patriots, the Boston Bruins, and the Boston Celtics, there is always a home team to root for, no matter the season.

Boston Red Sox

If it's baseball season, head to historic Fenway Park to catch a game (and if it's not, see below for info on tours). No seat is far from the action at this intimate 1912 stadium, the oldest ballpark in the major leagues.

Season is April through October.
4 Jersey St., 877-REDSOX-9 (733-7699)

redsox.com

New England Patriots

With five Super Bowl wins in the last sixteen years, the Patriots have proven they are a team to reckon with. Head to Gillette Stadium to see them in action, and if you're lucky, maybe you'll even catch New England's favorite QB Tom Brady tossing the pigskin (if he hasn't retired yet).

Season is August through January.
Gillette Stadium, 1 Patriot Pl., Foxborough

patriots.com

Boston Bruins

Boston is a hardcore hockey town, and the Bruins, one of the
National Hockey League's original six teams, is one of the
most storied franchises in North America. Head to TD Garden,
where Bobby Orr's goal in overtime during Game 4 of the 1970
Stanley Cup Final against the St. Louis Blues is still legend.
These days, cheer on stellar players like Tuukka Rask,
Patrice Bergeron, and Zdeno Chára.

Season is October through April.
TD Garden, 100 Legends Way, 617-624-2327

bruins.nhl.com

Boston Celtics

The "Gahden" is also home to the Boston Celtics, who still
have the most titles in NBA history. Boston's team hit it big
again in the 1980s, thanks to the Big Three (Larry Bird, Kevin
McHale, and Robert Parish) and most recently in 2008, thanks
to the New Big Three (Paul Pierce, Kevin Garnett, and Ray
Allen). Who knows what will happen next?
Don't miss a chance to see!

Season is October through April.
TD Garden, 100 Legends Way, 866-423-5849

nba.com/celtics

GO BEHIND THE SCENES
AT FENWAY PARK

Not a baseball fan? It doesn't matter. You should still take a tour of America's oldest Major League Baseball park, where the Red Sox have played since 1912. None of Boston's sporting venues can hold a candle to Fenway Park, which locals regard as a shrine. On the excellent guided tours, which the park offers year-round, you'll see where Ted Williams's famous 502-foot home run landed, learn about Pesky's Pole, enjoy the view from the world-famous Green Monster, which stands 37 feet, 2 inches high overlooking left field, and even get onto the hallowed ground of the field. After your visit, you can claim status as being part of "Red Sox Nation."

4 Jersey St., 617-226-6666
mlb.com/redsox/ballpark/tours

CHEER ON THE RUNNERS
AT THE BOSTON MARATHON

The Boston Marathon is one of the most prestigious—not to mention most challenging—marathons in the world. Organized by the Boston Athletic Association, the race is part of the World Marathon Majors series, the planet's six largest and most renowned marathons. Since 1897, runners have tackled the course, which starts somewhat gently for the first several miles but includes a series of brutal uphill climbs, culminating with "Heartbreak Hill" at Mile 20, a major hurdle for most.

Ask any marathoner and they'll tell you what helps get them through the tough race is the legions of cheering fans who stand all along the course with signs, water, and shouts of encouragement. The closer to the finish line, the bigger the crowds, and the more festive the atmosphere, but spectators are welcome everywhere on the route. Pick your spot and add your voice to the supporters. It's an awe-inspiring sight to witness the single-minded athletes run their hearts out.

Third Monday of April.

Start: Main St., Hopkinton
Finish: Boylston St. at Dartmouth St., Boston
baa.org

DIP AN OAR
IN THE CHARLES RIVER

Get a different perspective on the city from the water. The Charles River offers a wealth of activities, from kayaking to canoeing to splashing down in one of the city's ubiquitous and colorful Duck Boats. Other options include sailing, stand-up paddleboarding and taking a leisurely riverboat. Pirate ships more your thing? Yep, we've got one of those, too!

Duck Boats

Jump aboard Boston Duck Tours, which take place aboard World War II-style amphibious landing vehicles. The narrated tour swings by Boston's main sights, from the Massachusetts State House to Bunker Hill, and then heads straight into the Charles River.

617-267-3825

bostonducktours.com

Community Boating

Located near the Charles Street footbridge on the Esplanade, Community Boating offers sailboats, kayaks, and stand-up paddleboards for rent.

21 David G Mugar Way, 617-523-1038

community-boating.org

Charles Riverboat Company

Take a seventy-minute narrated sightseeing cruise along the Charles River for a laidback way to see the city. Architecture and sunset cruises are also available. Cruises depart from Lechmere Canal Park at the CambridgeSide mall.

10 CambridgeSide Pl., Cambridge, 617-621-3001

charlesriverboat.com/tours/charles-river-tours

RELAX
ON A HARBOR CRUISE

Several companies take passengers out on the harbor on all types of cruises, from dinner sails to dancing under the stars. It's a fantastic way to gain a new perspective of the city.

Boston Harbor Cruises

BHC offers themed cruises such as brunch, stargazing, historic, sunset, fireworks, and even cruises to view the USS *Constitution*.

One Long Wharf, 617-227-4321

bostonharborcruises.com/contact-us

Massachusetts Bay Lines

Set sail on *The Formidable*, a tall ship that sails around Boston Harbor. If you're not into pirate-themed cruises, the company offers regular tall ship sails, too.

60 Rowes Wharf, 617-542-8000

massbaylines.com/daily-boston-harbor-tour

Entertainment Cruises

This company runs the upscale *Spirit of Boston* and *Odyssey* ships in the harbor, with lunch, brunch, dinner, and dancing cruises.

Rowes Wharf, 800-700-0735

entertainmentcruises.com/our-ships

PLAY AROUND
ON LAWN ON D

This seasonal all-ages playground has something for everyone, from a full bar stocked with adult beverages for the twenty-one-plus crowd to a variety of lawn games like giant Connect Four that kids (and the young at heart) love to play. The 2.7-acre park, which is located adjacent to (and is operated by) the Boston Convention and Exhibition Center, is typically open from May through October and is free to enter.

The enclosed lawn features cool round swings that light up at night, a covered pavilion where both live acts and DJs play music, and a concession stand with typical barbecue favorites like hot dogs and burgers. There are also ping-pong tables, bocce courts, corn hole boards, temporary art installations, and special movie nights. I saw *Jaws* here one summer evening when the entire crowd knew all the dialogue and shouted out favorite lines ("You're gonna need a bigger boat," of course, was deafening.)

420 D St., 877-393-3393
signatureboston.com/lawn-on-d/community-activities/open-lawn

WATCH
THE HEAD OF THE CHARLES

This annual fall event brings out hordes of crowds who line the Charles River to cheer on sculling crew teams competing in the world-famous Head of the Charles Regatta, which has been held here since 1965. More than eleven thousand athletes of all ages, from their teens to their eighties, descend on the city to race in the globe's largest two-day rowing event.

This is definitely a lively spectator sport, with vendors setting up food and beer stands along both sides of the river. The Charles River's many bridges get packed with cheering fans, but they offer an excellent vantage point if you're willing to be crowded. It's much more relaxing to bring a picnic, some chairs, or a blanket; find a grassy spot on either bank; and enjoy the views of the rowers as they glide along.

Third weekend in October.
617-868-6200
hocr.org

TREK AROUND THE CITY
BY BIKE

Cycling is a great way to get an overview of Boston and cover a lot of ground in an active way. Boston's popular bike-share program, called Blue Bikes, has 1,800 bikes at two hundred stations located in Boston, Brookline, Cambridge, and Somerville. Riders can rent bikes 24/7, starting at $2.50 for a thirty-minute single ride to a ten-dollar pass, which gives access to a bike for two hours at a time in a twenty-four-hour period. You can download an app on your smartphone to rent bikes or purchase a pass at the stations.

bluebikes.com

TIP

If you'd rather have a tour guide, Urban AdvenTours offers guided bicycle tours around the city. Options include city view tours, Emerald Necklace tours, Fenway tours, sunset tours, and more.

103 Atlantic Ave., 800-979-3370
urbanadventours.com

CULTURE AND HISTORY

CHECK OUT
MORE THAN BOOKS
AT THE BOSTON PUBLIC LIBRARY

Among Boston's many historic and beautiful buildings, the main branch of the BPL is one of the more surprising. It's much more than a mere book repository. The nation's first free library began circulating books in 1854, and its main branch is now housed in a magnificent Renaissance Beaux-Arts Classicism building constructed in 1895. It houses world-class artworks and murals as well as a beautiful reading room that runs 218 feet long with a fifty-foot-high barrel-arch ceiling.

Upon walking through the main entrance, visitors are greeted by immense stone lions crafted by Louis Saint-Gaudens, a grand marble staircase, and murals painted by French artist Pierre Puvis de Chavannes depicting the nine muses. Upstairs, in the public areas leading to the fine-art, music, and rare-book collections, you'll find John Singer Sargent's mural series, *Triumph of Religion*. A Renaissance-style courtyard, complete with fountain, is an exact replica of the one in Rome's Palazzo della Cancelleria. Free art and architecture tours are offered daily—a perfect introduction to the library—or you can pick up a brochure and explore on your own.

700 Boylston St., 617-536-5400
bpl.org

· ·

TOUR TRINITY CHURCH

Trinity Church, one of the main anchors of Copley Square, is a must, whether you're a churchgoer or not (and this is a working church, not a museum). Dedicated in 1877, the church is a stunner, not to mention a daring architectural feat for the time. Since the Back Bay is basically filled-in wetlands, older buildings were constructed on thousands of submerged wooden pilings.

But when you're inside the gorgeous building, with its intricately carved woodwork, superb masonry, beautiful stained-glass windows, and breathtaking murals and artwork, you probably won't be thinking about what's far beneath your feet. The Richardsonian Romanesque design is named after its architect, Henry Hobson Richardson, and Trinity is his masterpiece. Take a guided tour (or self-guide) to learn about the building's history. Tours are free on Sundays immediately after the service. Otherwise, it's seven dollars.

206 Clarendon St., 617-536-0944
trinitychurchboston.org

DELVE INTO THE ARTS
AT THE MUSEUM OF FINE ARTS, BOSTON

There are a few ways to approach this massive museum, home to more than half a million objects ranging from ancient Egyptian artifacts to modern-day artwork: 1) plan so you can see what's important to you; 2) come with an open mind and wander at will, taking in what you can; or 3) hop on a free guided tour (included with admission) to check out the museum's biggest stars. You can visit the museum's website in advance to make a game plan.

That said, the Art of the Americas wing is a great place to start. With sixteen thousand objects in forty-nine galleries across four floors, the wing includes such highlights as early colonial New England decorative arts and paintings, with John Singleton Copley's famous portrait of Paul Revere and the silversmith's Sons of Liberty Bowl; John Singer Sargent's *The Daughters of Edward Darley Boit*; and Frida Kahlo's *Dos Mujeres* (*Salvadora y Herminia*). Tickets are pricey, but they are good for two visits within ten days, plus a discount at the nearby Isabella Stewart Gardner Museum.

465 Huntington Ave., 617-267-9300
mfa.org

EMBRACE AN ECCENTRIC
AT THE ISABELLA STEWART GARDNER MUSEUM

Who doesn't love a free spirit? In 1860, Isabella Stewart came to Boston from New York to marry John Lowell Gardner, one of Boston's leading citizens. "Mrs. Jack," as she became known, quickly set about disregarding societal norms of the day, building a gorgeous Venetian palazzo, complete with a beautiful interior courtyard, to hold her ever-growing collection of art. She also entertained such leading lights as Henry James and Edith Wharton. Masterpieces in her collection include Titan's *Rape of Europa*, Giotto's *Presentation of Christ Child in the Temple*, and John Singer Sargent's *El Jaleo*, among others.

Today, the museum is exactly as she left it, as she stipulated in her will. It feels as though she could sweep through the door even to this day. However, a much-needed addition, completed in 2012, includes a music hall, exhibit space, and conservation labs, where artwork can be repaired and preserved.

25 Evans Way, 617-566-1401
gardnermuseum.org

GO MODERN
AT THE INSTITUTE OF CONTEMPORARY ART

Not only is the ICA home to cutting-edge art, but the building itself can considered a piece of art in its own right. The stunning glass-walled cantilevered building, opened in 2006, sits right on the edge of the Boston waterfront, offering breathtaking views both inside and out. Since it was founded in 1936, the ICA has been instrumental in identifying or showcasing the most important artists of the day, such as Edvard Munch, Andy Warhol, Laurie Anderson, and Roy Lichtenstein. More recently, it has been pivotal in the careers of artists like Bill Viola, Kara Walker, Cindy Sherman, Shepard Fairey, and Rashaun Mitchell.

One of the joys of visiting the ICA is that there is always something new and exciting going on, including ever-changing exhibitions, live music and dance performances, provocative film and digital media selections, talks, tours, family activities, and teen programming. You're always guaranteed a great evening at the museum's First Friday series, which features anything from guest DJs to virtual reality art pop-up installations.

25 Harbor Shore Dr., 617-478-3100
icaboston.org

GO FISHING
FOR THE SACRED COD
AT THE STATE HOUSE

The golden-domed Massachusetts State House is an important building for many reasons. The land it sits on was originally used as John Hancock's cow pasture. It was designed by Charles Bulfinch and completed in 1798. The cornerstone was laid by Samuel Adams in 1795, and a copper dome was installed by Paul Revere in 1802 (later to be covered in gold). Senators, state representatives, and the governor conduct the Commonwealth's business here.

But one of my favorite things about the State House is that it is also home to the Sacred Cod, which visitors can spy in the House of Representatives Chamber on a free tour. The almost five-foot-long wooden cod, which symbolizes the importance of the salt cod industry to the area, was first installed in the Old State House in 1784. The one you see today is actually the third cod. Cod number one was destroyed in a fire and cod number two was lost (maybe destroyed by the British!). Cod number three even disappeared for a few days in 1933 as a prank, but it was returned. It has to be Boston's most unlikely fish story!

24 Beacon St., 617-727-3676
malegislature.gov/StateHouse/Tour

GAZE IN WONDER
AT TIFFANY WINDOWS

The Arlington Street Church in Back Bay, built in 1861, is the oldest church in the neighborhood and is said to be home to the largest collection of Tiffany stained-glass windows of any church in the world, with sixteen beautifully crafted scenes representing religious themes. Installed between 1898 and 1929, the windows are simply breathtaking and definitely worth a visit. The church still has an active congregation, but visitors are welcome to take self-guided audio tours or sign up for a docent-led tour.

351 Boylston St., 617-536-7050
ascboston.org

EXPLORE BOSTON'S BLACK HERITAGE TRAIL

The Freedom Trail isn't the only trail to follow in Boston. For a trip through the city's African American history and legacy, head to Beacon Hill. You can either pick up maps and site brochures and start at the Abiel Smith School, built in 1835 to educate black children, or download a map to do a self-guided tour. Included among the fourteen sites are the Robert Gould Shaw Memorial on Beacon Street; the Lewis and Harriet Hayden House, a station on the Underground Railroad and a meeting place for abolitionists; and the African Meeting House, built at the turn of the nineteenth century by free blacks and the oldest surviving building of its kind in the United States.

46 Joy St., 617-742-5415
nps.gov/boaf

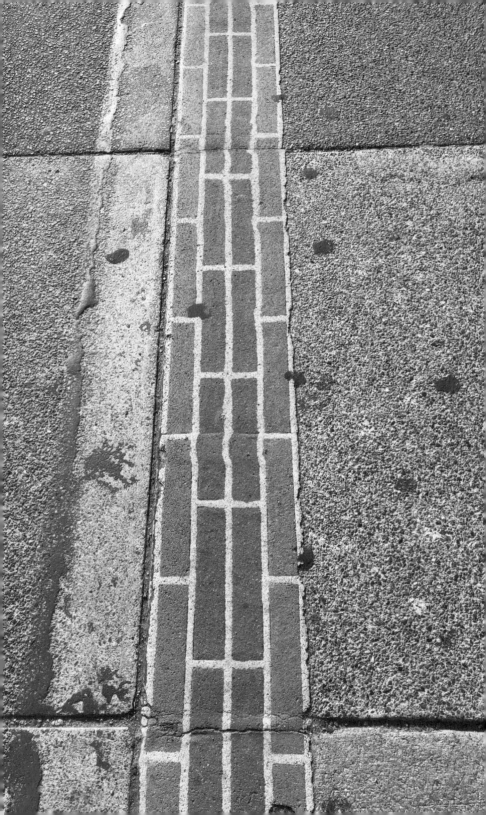

FOLLOW THE RED BRICK (AND SOMETIMES PAINTED) FREEDOM TRAIL

Along with the Swan Boats, the Freedom Trail is another ubiquitous attraction on the front of countless guidebooks and in top-ten lists about Boston. There's a reason for that. Actually, there are several. First up, it's free. Just plant yourself on the red brick trail (sometimes it's a painted red line) and start walking. Along the 2.5-mile trail, you'll encounter sixteen of the city's most important historic sights (along with a ton of other places to rest, eat, drink, and visit), including Faneuil Hall, Old North Church, the Paul Revere House, King's Chapel, and the Bunker Hill Monument. Some of these places do charge fees.

You can start the tour wherever you like, but if you want to go in an orderly fashion, start from Boston Common, where you can pick up handy maps at the Visitor Information Center kiosk (or you can download one). You can also sign up for a free guided tour given by the National Park Service that leaves from Faneuil Hall. Another option is to pay for a tour with the Freedom Trail Foundation, where eighteenth-century costumed guides lead the way. No matter how you choose to explore the trail, don't forget sturdy walking shoes! Boston's cobblestones and uneven streets can be brutal on your feet.

Starting point: Boston Common Visitor Information Center
139 Tremont St., 617-357-8300, thefreedomtrail.org

DIVE INTO THE SEA (WITHOUT GETTING WET) AT THE NEW ENGLAND AQUARIUM

Appropriately located right on the waterfront, the New England Aquarium is one of Boston's more popular attractions. Its showstopper is its four-story, two-hundred-thousand-gallon Giant Ocean Tank, one of the largest of its kind in the world. Fun fact: the tank was built first, then the rest of the aquarium was constructed around it! It's impossible not be mesmerized by all the sea creatures swimming around as you meander up the winding ramp leading to the top. My personal favorite is Myrtle, the green sea turtle, who has lived at the aquarium since 1970. More than one thousand other animals live alongside Myrtle, including moray eels, sharks, barracuda, and all sorts of colorful reef fishes. Do yourself a big favor and purchase your tickets in advance online. Weekend, summer, and holiday lines can be miserable.

1 Central Wharf, 617-973-5200

neaq.org

FOLLOW
IN PAUL REVERE'S FOOTSTEPS AT OLD NORTH CHURCH

"One if by land, and two if by sea."

No doubt you've heard this refrain before (hundreds of times if you grew up in the United States), so why not see exactly where Paul Revere and the sexton Robert Newman managed to signal the departure by water of the British regulars to Lexington and Concord on the night of April 18, 1775. Old North Church, built in 1723, is Boston's oldest standing church building, and to this day it has an active Episcopal congregation.

You can drop in for services, but for a more comprehensive look at history, take the Behind the Scenes tour, where you get to visit the bell-ringing chamber and the crypt. As you head up the same stairs Paul Revere trod, I dare you not to feel a sense of awe. Down below in the crypt, thirty-seven tombs serve as the final resting place of 1,100 souls, the most famous of whom is Samuel Nicholson, the first captain of the USS *Constitution*. Inside the church, sit in a box pew (when there are no services) and listen to a short presentation about the founding of Old North, the lantern story, and the church's role in the American Revolution.

193 Salem St., 617-858-8231
oldnorth.com

• •

CLIMB ABOARD
THE USS *CONSTITUTION*

After a twenty-six-month restoration, the USS *Constitution* returned to her usual berth in the Charlestown Navy Yard in 2017. Better known as "Old Ironsides," the USS *Constitution* is the oldest commissioned ship in the U.S. fleet. She was launched on October 21, 1797, as part of the nation's new navy. Her hull was made of live oak, the toughest wood grown in North America, and her bottom was sheathed in copper provided by Paul Revere. The nickname "Old Ironsides" was coined during the War of 1812, when shots from the British warship *Guerrière* appeared to bounce off her hull. In forty-two engagements, she never lost a battle—an impressive record.

Today, she serves as America's Ship of State, and visitors are welcome. You can explore the top three decks, and the crew is happy to explain all matters of naval history and ship facts and figures. Don't miss the USS *Constitution* Museum just next door for more info and hands-on exhibits that kids (and many adults) love. Who doesn't want to see if they can aim a cannon accurately or haul a billy goat—named Billie—on board?

Charlestown Navy Yard, 55 Constitution Rd., 617-242-7511
navy.mil/local/constitution

TIP

The USS *Constitution* usually holds a lottery in the spring for one hundred or so lucky winners (and their guests) who get to join the ship on its annual July Fourth turnaround on Boston Harbor. Believe it or not, I entered one year and won, so I know it's possible!

TOSS TEA
AT THE BOSTON TEA PARTY
SHIPS & MUSEUM

Sometimes all of Boston's history and historical sites can seem overwhelming, perhaps even dry, but not so at this hands-on interactive museum, where you can toss (fake) tea overboard, climb around replica ships, and converse with period actors about colonial issues.

Exhibits at the museum, which is located on Griffin's Wharf (close to where the actual Tea Party occurred on December 16, 1773) include cool 3-D holograms, talking portraits, and even the Robinson Tea Chest, one of two original tea chests known to exist. To date, two of the three ships have been recreated, the *Beaver II* and the *Eleanor*, which you can explore at will. The third ship, the *Dartmouth*, is still a work in progress. Don't skip having a cup of tea in Abigail's Tea Room, which has one of the best views of the harbor around.

306 Congress St., 866-955-0667
bostonteapartyship.com

TIME TRAVEL TO 1935
AT THE MAPPARIUM

Located in the Mary Baker Eddy Library, this three-story, stained glass globe never fails to elicit wonder. Designed by the architect of the Christian Science Publishing Society building, Chester Lindsay Churchill, the globe depicts the world as it was in 1935, offering a glimpse into the not-too-distant past.

A World of Ideas, a presentation with words, music and LED lights, is part of the experience. There's also a complementary exhibit called *Mapparium: An Inside View*, featuring letters, documents, and artifacts detailing the construction, history, and significance of the Mapparium. One of the coolest features of the globe is that it is also a "whispering gallery." Stand at one end of the gallery while a friend stands at the other. Whisper something, and your friend will be the only one to hear it. Conversely, stand in the center, under the North Star, speak in a normal voice, and it sounds like you're being amplified. Three times every hour, visitors are permitted inside to check it out.

200 Massachusetts Ave., 617-450-7000
mbelibrary.org

TAKE A TOUR
OF THE BOSTON ATHENÆUM

Founded in 1807, the Boston Athenæum is one of the oldest independent libraries in the country. Though it is membership-based and public access is limited, you can visit some of its sacred places, such as the Norma Jean Calderwood Gallery, which features three exhibitions per year. The changing shows include objects from the Athenæum's extensive collections, as well as from other institutions. But to really see all there is, you'll need to take a guided tour, where you'll get to see the gorgeous fifth-floor Reading Room, with its two levels of antique books, high windows and amazing artwork. The library is home to treasures like George Washington's private library; the King's Chapel Library, sent from England by William III in 1698; portraits by John Singer Sargent; and pastels by John Singleton Copley.

10½ Beacon St., 617-227-0270
bostonathenaeum.org

CLIMB, CLIMB, CLIMB
THE BUNKER HILL MONUMENT

The first major battle of the American Revolution took place on Breed's Hill on July 17, 1775. So why did Boston commemorate the battle (which the Americans lost, by the way), with a monument called Bunker Hill? Originally, the Battle of Bunker Hill was supposed to take place on Bunker Hill (which is about half a mile away from the monument), but it actually took place on Breed's Hill, which is where the monument was placed. We just couldn't let go of the original name. Got it?

Names aside, and despite our loss, the British were the bigger losers here, sacrificing nearly half of their 2,200 men. The American casualties numbered between four and six hundred. Started in 1825 and completed in 1842, the 221-foot-tall granite obelisk offers fabulous views from its observatory, though you have to work for it by climbing 294 steps to the top (no, there's no elevator!). Free tickets are required to visit. Pick them up at the Bunker Hill Museum (located across the street) in advance.

Monument Sq.
nps.gov/bost/historyculture/bhm.htm

RIDE THE RAILS
ON MBTA

Boston is home to so many firsts, so why shouldn't public transit be one? Since 1897, Bostonians have been able to enjoy riding underground on subway cars, avoiding the heinous traffic that has been a problem forever. The Tremont Street subway opened that year as North America's first subway tunnel. It is still in use today, connecting Government Center, Park Street, and the Boylston stations.

FUN FACT

We call our tickets for the subway "Charlie Cards," all due to a clever campaign song written in 1949 called "Charlie on the MTA." It tells the story of a subway rider named Charlie who got stuck on an endless train ride underneath the streets of Boston because he was unable to pay the exit fare. Later, the Kingston Trio recorded a version of it that hit the Billboard charts. In 2004, the MBTA took the name for its fare system.

PAY YOUR RESPECTS
AT THE GRANARY BURYING GROUND

In the heart of downtown, this historic cemetery seems out of place among the bustling traffic and hordes of tourists and shoppers, but the 1660 graveyard is home to some of our country's most illustrious names. You'll find the graves of John Hancock, Paul Revere, James Otis, and Samuel Adams here. There's also a grave marker for the victims of the Boston Massacre and a plaque marking the tomb of Robert Treat Paine, the third signer of the Declaration of Independence. And while you can see 2,300 markers, far more people are buried here, with best estimates being around five thousand. This is one of the stops on the Freedom Trail, but even if you don't do the whole trail, this is one you shouldn't miss.

Tremont St.
thefreedomtrail.org/freedom-trail/granary-burying-ground.shtml

DREAM OF SUGARPLUMS
AT THE BOSTON BALLET

Every year, the city's premier dance company, the Boston Ballet, performs the classic ballet *The Nutcracker* at the sumptuous Boston Opera House to the delight of little girls and boys (and grown-ups) dreaming of a magical Christmas. It is an annual ritual for many families during the holidays.

If you don't know the story line (is that even possible?), the Cliff Notes version is that the tale is based on the book *The Nutcracker and the Mouse King*, written by E. T. A. Hoffmann in 1816. It tells the story of a young German girl who falls asleep under the tree on Christmas Eve with her favorite toy, a nutcracker in the shape of a soldier. When the clock strikes midnight, magical things begin to happen. The Boston Ballet dazzles audiences with colorful costumes, snow flurries, a mouse army, and Arabian dancers. And, of course, the 1892 score by Tchaikovsky never fails to delight. The company has much more than *The Nutcracker* in its repertoire, performing various world-class classical and modern works over the year.

19 Clarendon St., 617-695-6955
bostonballet.org

PAY HOMAGE
TO CAMELOT

If you are a fan of the Kennedys, or of history, or of politics and government in general, then you should make a beeline for Columbia Point, just past the campus of the University of Massachusetts-Boston. Both the excellent John F. Kennedy Presidential Library and Museum and the Edward M. Kennedy Institute for the U.S. Senate are located here. These men, two of Massachusetts's favorite sons, both had an undeniably powerful effect on American politics.

At the JFK Museum, a gorgeous building designed by I. M. Pei, check out Kennedy's presidential papers, a plethora of Kennedy memorabilia (including a re-creation of his desk in the Oval Office) and his twenty-six-foot sailboat. There's also a permanent display on the late Jacqueline Kennedy Onassis. The neighboring institute focuses on politics today, with an excellent and accurate reproduction of the U.S. Senate Chamber. Visitors get the chance to become "Senators-in-Training" and tackle current issues.

John F. Kennedy Presidential Library and Museum, Columbia Point
617-514-1600
jfklibrary.org

Edward M. Kennedy Institute, 210 Morrissey Blvd.
617-740-7000
emkinstitute.org

EXPLORE
HARVARD SQUARE

The beating heart of Cambridge is without a doubt Harvard Square, home to Harvard University, of course, but also to any number of unique shops, independent bookstores, cool arthouses, and all sorts of great people-watching cafés and restaurants. Start with the iconic Out of Town News, a kiosk in the center of the square, which has been selling newspapers and magazines from around the world for decades. Who says print is dead? Another local mainstay is the Harvard Book Store, a favorite with professors, students, and readers alike for the past eighty years. Certainly, Harvard's world-renowned museums are worth a visit, but simply wandering the leafy streets checking out historic homes is just as fun.

Cambridge

TOUR
HARVARD YARD

No visit to Cambridge, just across the Charles River from Boston, is complete without a visit to famous Harvard University, the nation's oldest school of higher learning. Enter through one of its storied gates and take in the Old Yard at your leisure, or sign up for a free tour, where student guides will assail you with tales about the campus and the story of the "statue of three lies."

Daniel Chester French's iconic statue of John Harvard, located in front of University Hall, has an inscription reading "John Harvard, Founder, 1638," not one item of which is true. Harvard University was actually established as the New College in 1636. It got its new name when John Harvard died in Charlestown in 1638, leaving a portion of his estate and his library of more than four hundred books to the school. And finally, there are no known portraits of the man, so when French created the statue almost 250 years after Harvard's death, he used a model (Sherman Hoar, who later in life became a congressman). No matter. Do what every other visitor and student does and rub the statue's toe for good luck!

Cambridge, 617-495-1000
harvard.edu

GET GLASSY-EYED
AT HARVARD'S COLLECTION
OF GLASS MODELS

Harvard's Museum of Natural History is home to two astonishing collections of works created by Czech glass artisans Leopold Blaschka and his son Rudolf, who crafted stunningly lifelike glass models of sea creatures and flowers over a span of fifty years in the late nineteenth and early twentieth centuries. The Ware Collection of Blaschka Glass Models of Plants includes more than four thousand models, representing more than 830 plant species. Incredibly detailed, the models were commissioned by Harvard in 1886 for use in the classroom and for public display. Before they made the flowers, however, the Blaschkas were transforming glass into lifelike models of marine animals. These were commissioned by universities and museums throughout the world during the nineteenth century.

It is well worth your time to check out both the Glass Flowers and Sea Creatures in Glass exhibits. I guarantee that your jaw will drop and you will find it hard to believe that the delicate tulips, orchids, irises, jellyfish, octopus, and tentacled squid are not the real things.

26 Oxford St., Harvard Square, 617-495-3045
hmnh.harvard.edu

MEANDER AROUND MIT

You may not have been admitted to MIT, but that shouldn't stop you from taking a stroll around the campus anyway. It's home to some of the most creative architecture and amazing sculptures in the area, with the added bonus of being entirely free to enjoy. Of the more than fifty sights to check out, the don't-miss ones include buildings by Alvar Aalto, Eduardo Catalano, I. M. Pei, Frank Gehry, and Eero Saarinen, as well as sculptures, murals, and paintings by Alexander Calder, Henry Moore, Anish Kapoor, Pablo Picasso, and Louise Nevelson.

Visit MIT's website to download a map or to access an audio guide, which opens appropriately enough with an introduction by actor Leonard Nimoy. You can also download the MIT app on your smart phone.

Cambridge, 617-253-4680
listart.mit.edu/collections/public-art-collection

TIP

Check out the MIT Museum, which features a variety of science and technology topics. Don't miss the most comprehensive collection of holograms in the world. And for crazy cool drinks, head to the nearby Café ArtScience, where the bartenders are more like alchemists, whipping up creative potions.

SHOPPING AND FASHION

ENJOY A TRIPLE THREAT
AT FANEUIL HALL MARKETPLACE

You can be forgiven if you confuse Faneuil Hall Marketplace with Faneuil Hall, or even with Quincy Market, since they are all in a cluster and many locals often just refer to the whole area as Faneuil Hall. Shoppers will want to go to Faneuil Hall Marketplace to find a slew of independent shops, pushcarts with Boston-centric goods, and lots of buskers and street performers entertaining the crowds just outside. Quincy Market is where you'll find food stalls packed with an enormous variety of vendors cooking up everything from chowder to pizza to lobster rolls. Historic Faneuil Hall, aka "The Cradle of Liberty," is where all sorts of political and civic events have been held throughout the centuries, including speeches by Samuel Adams, George Washington, Susan B. Anthony, Bill Clinton, and Ted Kennedy. Make a day of it in the complex, shopping, eating, and learning!

4 South Market Building, 617-523-1300
faneuilhallmarketplace.com

CHECK OUT THE OLD AND THE NEW
AT HAYMARKET

Since 1820, this open-air market, where vendors loudly extol the virtues of their fresh fruits and vegetables to hordes of locals, has been a mainstay in the city. Located just next to Faneuil Hall and open only on Fridays and Saturdays, it's a madhouse of wheeling and dealing and a hoot to check out. Pick up some berries or other fruit for a snack, then look on the ground for the fun bronze art installation celebrating the market. Tip: Don't touch the merchandise! The vendors will help you with your order and will not be pleased, loudly, if you don't let them.

Blackstone St. (between Hanover and North Sts.)
haymarketboston.org

BROWSE INDOORS
AT BOSTON PUBLIC MARKET

Slightly less chaotic and open daily is the indoor Boston Public Market, a great spot to pick up locally produced items (as well as to eat on the spot). More than thirty-five New England artisans and food producers sell everything from fresh food to prepared meals to local crafts and other specialty items. Everything sold at the market is produced or originates in New England. You can also pick up pointers at The KITCHEN, where cooking classes and demos are often held.

100 Hanover St., 617-973-4909
bostonpublicmarket.org

GO UPSCALE
ON NEWBURY STREET

Eight-block-long Newbury Street is Boston's fanciest shopping area, chockablock with high-end stores alternating with restaurants, bars, cafés, and for some reason, more hair salons than seem reasonable for such a small area. Shopaholics will be happy to know that branches of Barbour, Chanel, Diane von Furstenberg, Longchamp, Shreve, Crump & Low, and other top brands are here, as well as a slew of independent boutique shops. In warm weather, the street's outdoor bar and restaurant patios are the places to see and be seen, so you may want to dress sharp! Just a block away is Boylston Street, where you can find even more shops and restaurants.

newbury-st.com

GET WICKED
AT NEWBURY COMICS

Not everything on Newbury Street is super chichi. More than any other shop in Boston, Newbury Comics, which has been around since 1978, has been the face of the city's pop culture, with music, silly gifts, and of course, comic books on its shelves. The independently owned retailer, which uses the tagline "A Wicked Good Time," also has played host to acts like Aerosmith and The Cars over the years, with record release parties and special events. You'll find music in every iteration, from cassettes tapes to newly pressed vinyl, as well as posters, T-shirts, houseware items, action figures and more, in the eclectic shop. Though it now has more than two dozen stores in New England and New York, it retains its sassy Boston-centric sense of humor.

332 Newbury St., 617-236-4930
newburycomics.com

EXPLORE
BOSTON'S MAIN STREETS

Boston is a city of very distinct neighborhoods, each with a different character and flavor. The city's Main Streets program, a nonprofit network designed to help local businesses survive and thrive in their commercial districts, shines a light on twenty neighborhoods that are definitely worth checking out. Small independent shops, locally owned restaurants, farmers markets, pop-up shops and events, annual festivals, and much more await urban explorers. Best of all, each one is easily accessible via public transportation, too!

bostonmainstreets.org

GET ARTSY
AT THE SoWa OPEN MARKET

Located in SoWa, an area of the South End south of Washington Street, the Open Market is a fantastic collection of more than 175 local artists, farmers, food trucks, brewers, and musicians based in one sprawling location. Now in its fifteenth year, the Sunday event, which runs May through October, has something for everyone. Looking for something unique to hang on your wall? Check. Looking for gorgeous handmade jewelry? Check. Looking for a local beer? Check. It's great browsing and people watching, plus special programs like yoga, flower arranging, and painting are frequently offered.

530 Harrison Ave., 857-362-7692
sowaboston.com/sowa-open-market

TREASURE HUNT
AT THE SoWa VINTAGE MARKET

Keep going past the Open Market and you'll discover the indoor, and open year-round, Vintage Market, where you can hunt for antiques, collectibles, clothing, art, and one-of-a-kind items you'd never find in a regular shop. Whether you're looking for a hard-to-find comic book, a leather jacket with fringe trim, or the perfect silver serving dish, chances are good you can find it here. Vendors rotate in and out, so there's always something new to check out. It's like a big, cool treasure hunt, and you'll never know what gem you might uncover on any given Sunday.

450 Harrison Ave (Downstairs)
sowavintagemkt.com

BOUTIQUE HOP
ON CHARLES STREET

Charles Street in Beacon Hill, just across from Boston Common, is packed end to end with adorable shops, from antique emporiums to independent boutiques, all of which are worthy of a browse. Here's a list of the not-to-miss shops. If you need a break, there are plenty of places to eat and drink along the street, too.

Flat of the Hill
(boutique gift shop with
jewelry, handbags, etc.)
60 Charles St.
617-619-9977
flatofthehill.com

Black Ink
(stationery, cards, custom
wrapping paper)
101 Charles St.
617-723-3883
blackinkboston.com

Savenor's Market
(specialty food market)
160 Charles St.
617-723-6328
savenorsmarket.com

**Twentieth Century
Limited**
(vintage costume jewelry,
hats)
73 Charles St.
617-742-1031
boston-vintagejewelry
.com

Danish Country
(Scandinavian & Asian
antiques)
138 Charles St.
617-227-1804
danishcountry.net

Helen's Leather
(boots, coats, bags, belts)
110 Charles St.
617-742-2077
helensleather.com

NRO Kids
(boutique children's
clothing)
126 Charles St.
617-500-2408
northriveroutfitter.com

Holiday
(designer and handmade
clothes)
53 Charles St.
617-973-9730
holidayboutique.net

SPY OUT A HIDDEN STORE
AT BODEGA

I'm a sucker for a secret bar, restaurant, or shop, and Bodega, located behind a door (disguised as a soda machine) in what looks like a convenience store, fits the bill nicely. The soda machine/door magically slides open as you approach it. Inside, you discover a high-end, very selective menswear store of fancy footwear, snappy clothes, and hip accessories from more than one hundred brands. A casual passerby would never know what Bodega is—the storefront windows look like any other cluttered shop, with sodas, laundry detergent, canned goods, and other sundry items on the shelves—and there's no sign, so you need to keep a sharp eye out to find it.

6 Clearway St.
shop.bdgastore.com

BUY A BOOK
AT TRIDENT BOOKSELLERS AND CAFÉ

This Newbury Street store, temporarily closed at publication time due to fire, has been a gathering spot since 1984, with a large selection of new and used books, unique and hard-to-find magazines, and funky gifts, plus an excellent café, where you can read to your heart's content while sipping on a glass of wine or snacking on sweet potato fries. Host to all sorts of literary events, from book readings to author Q&As to book clubs, the closure, even temporary, is a big loss to the neighborhood, but until it reopens, the shop is operating online and at special events around town. It can use all the support it can get, so keep checking on its status and order some books!

338 Newbury St., 617-267-8688
tridentbookscafe.com

BROWSE FOR HOURS
AT THE BRATTLE BOOK SHOP

Another not-to-miss nirvana for booklovers is the historic Brattle Book Shop, which is packed floor to ceiling with books of every type, from *New York Times* best-sellers to nineteenth-century fiction. Founded in 1825, the bookstore has been owned and operated by the same family since 1949. There are two floors of general used books and a third floor of rare and antiquarian books. The store houses a mind-boggling collection of 250,000-plus books, maps, prints, and postcards, so be prepared to take your time to explore.

9 West St., 617-542-0210
brattlebookshop.com

ACTIVITIES
BY SEASON

SPRING

Down a Dog at Sullivan's, 6

Check Out the Old and the New at Haymarket, 117

Get Artsy at the SoWa Open Market, 122

Enjoy a Triple Threat at Faneuil Hall Marketplace, 116

Cheer On the Runners at the Boston Marathon, 75

SUMMER

Watch a Play under the Stars at Shakespeare on the Common, 40

Swim and Sip at the Rooftop Colonnade Pool, 27

Brunch on the Rooftop at the Taj, 32

Ride a Giant Swan in the Public Garden, 58

Celebrate America's Birthday at Boston Harborfest with
the Boston Pops, 51

Head to the Source at Island Creek Oysters, 5

FALL

WINTER

SUGGESTED
ITINERARIES

CLASSIC BOSTON

Down a Dog at Sullivan's, 6

Check Out the Old and the New at Haymarket, 117

Taste a Sweet Piece of History at Parker House, 19

Snap a Photo on Acorn Street, 63

Order a Slice at Santarpio's, 20

Enjoy a Triple Threat at Faneuil Hall Marketplace, 116

Ride the Rails on MBTA, 104

HISTORY BUFFS

Pay Your Respects at the Granary Burying Ground, 106

Follow the Red Brick (and Sometimes Painted) Freedom Trail, 95

Explore Boston's Black Heritage Trail, 93

Follow in Paul Revere's Footsteps at Old North Church, 97

Climb, Climb, Climb the Bunker Hill Monument, 103

Climb Aboard the USS *Constitution*, 98

FOODIE HEAVEN

Dine in Elegance at Eastern Standard, 7

Croon a Little at the Sinatra Brunch at Lucky's, 42

Dig In to a Steak at Grill 23, 8

• •

• •

NIGHTTIME FUN

EXCITING EVENTS

STOCK UP ON SOUVENIRS

SECRET BOSTON

INDEX

• •

• •

• •